NORTH EAST CUMBERLAND

Roy Millward and Adrian Robinson

Contents

MACMILLAN

First published 1972   Reprinted 1974

Published by
MACMILLAN EDUCATION LIMITED
Basingstoke and London
Companies and representatives
throughout the world

Printed in Great Britain by
FLETCHER AND SON LTD
Norwich

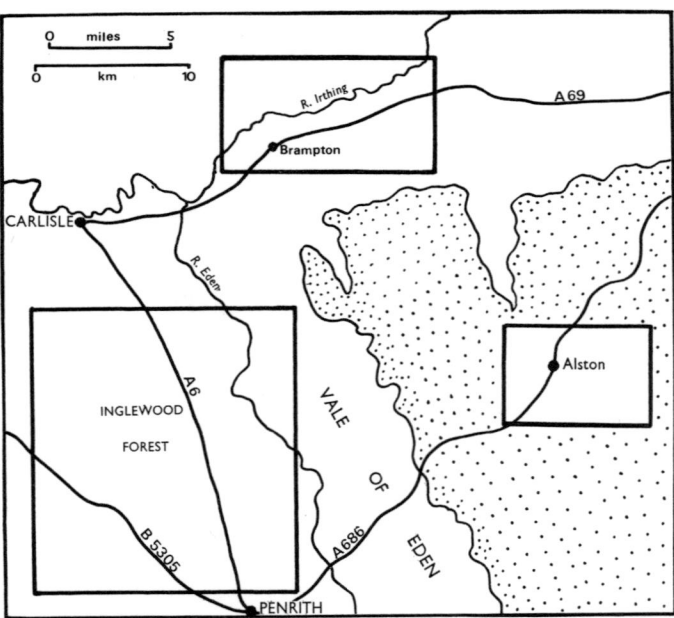

This booklet forms part of a larger volume, *Cumbria*, one of *The Landscapes of Britain* series. It consists of three sample studies which seek to explain in depth some of the distinctive themes in the history and geography of the area. A section of the Roman Wall where it runs close to the Irthing Valley has been chosen to illustrate some of the features of this finest standing monument of Roman Britain. A landscape which can be traced back to the medieval period forms the basis of the study of Inglewood Forest while the recent past is considered in the analysis of the lead-mining landscape around Alston.

Part Two   Individual Studies
1 The Irthing Valley – the Country of the Roman Wall

Certain regions of England derive some of their most characteristic features from a single period of history. Some of the most striking objects in the topography of the Welsh Marches appeared in the two centuries that followed the Norman Conquest, but in the border lands of northern Cumberland the mind must probe back into a remoter period of time, the four centuries of Roman occupation, to understand the present landscape. Where the deep grass-green trough of the Irthing Valley stretches between Brampton (5261) and Gilsland (6366), some of the most impressive features of the landscape owe their origin to the demarcation of a Roman frontier, early in the second century A.D. Perhaps even more astonishing is the persistence of Roman topographical features centuries after their creation. Farms stand on the line of Hadrian's Wall, Roman roads partly underlie the present communication pattern and the distinctive square-cut stones of the Roman masons have been re-used in field boundaries and countless humble domestic buildings down the centuries.

The Topography of the Roman Frontier in the Irthing Valley

Between Brampton and Gilsland we can study the archaeology of the Roman Wall in great variety and over a wide band of country (Figs. 1*a* and 1*b*). The earliest relics of the Roman occupation lie mainly to the south of the River Irthing, and belong to the years of the primary conquest of northern Britain between A.D. 78 and 85, when Agricola thrust the first network of roads and forts into the central lowlands of Scotland. A road, Stanegate, was built to join the Roman centres of Corbridge and Carlisle. It ran through this district on the high ground to the south of the winding gorge of the Irthing. Shreds of the road can still be traced, enough to reveal the line of its difficult course across the heads of the deep tributary streams that run into the Irthing from the south. For instance, almost a mile (one and a half kilometres) of this earliest Roman road can be followed across the edge of the moors to the south-east of Gilsland (6465). Fragments of the route appear at two places near Naworth Park, where an elaborate embankment and cutting takes a winding section of the road across the head of the ravine of the Carling Gill (576633).

The history of the Stanegate illustrates the changing value of communications down the centuries. Today the line of the road is all but lost for a large part of the

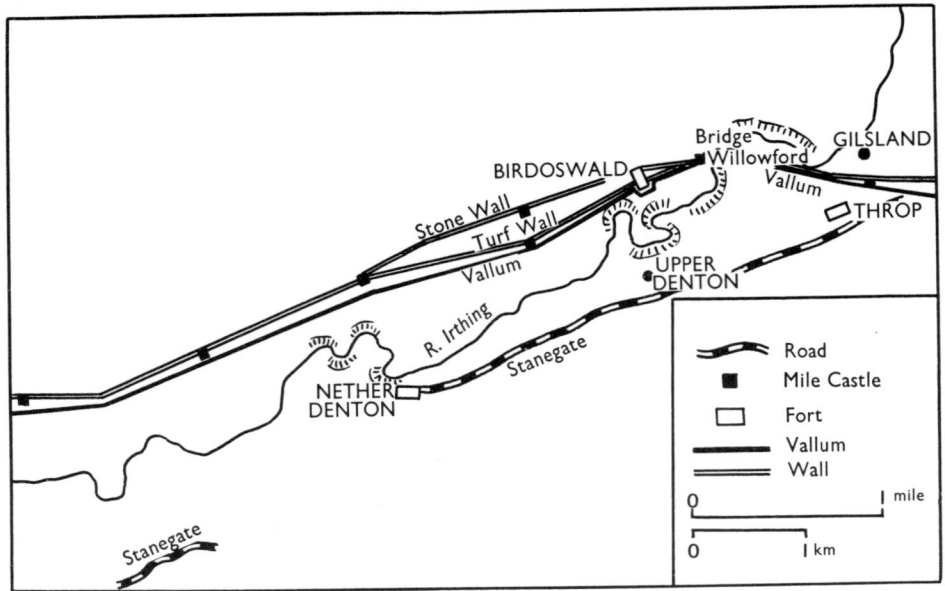

Fig. 1a *Features of the Roman Wall country around Birdoswald*

section to the south of the Irthing, although in the Middle Ages the Stanegate had acted as the main traffic line between Newcastle and Carlisle. It was superseded in the 1750s by the building of the military road between the two regional capitals of the north. The directness of this eighteenth-century route across the moors provides a deceptive feature of the topography in a countryside that is so rich with Roman remains.

The first forts of the northern frontier were located close to the line of the Stanegate in the three decades before the building of Hadrian's Wall. The most certain proof of an early fort has been obtained from the hill to the south of the Irthing, at Nether Denton, (596646) where the church and rectory now stand. In the field immediately to the south of the church a rampart and ditch may still be faintly recognised.

When the northern frontier was replanned under the Emperor Hadrian, new forts were built along the line of the Stanegate. Throp (632659) stands overlooking

Fig. 1b *The section of the Roman Wall north of Brampton* .

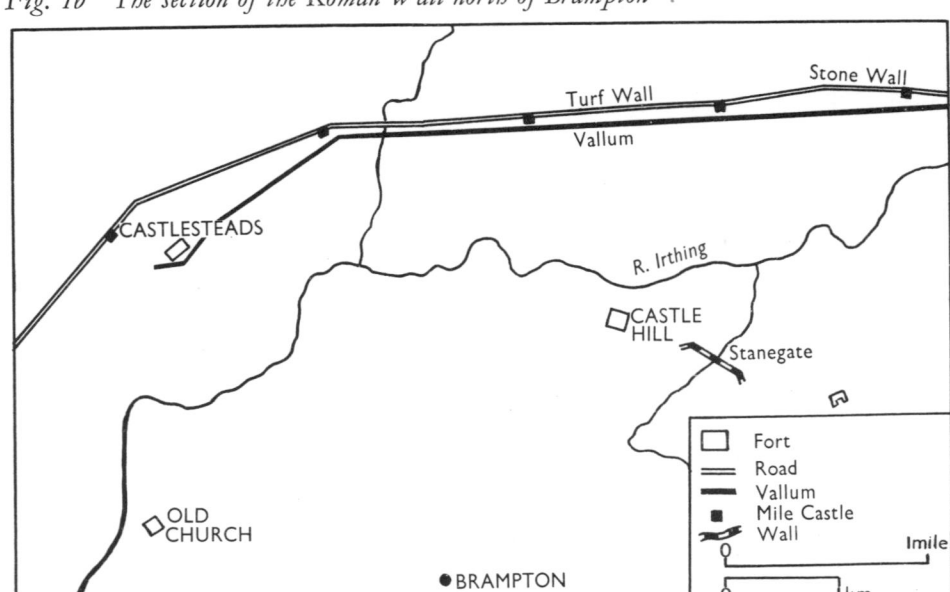

the deep narrow valley of the Poltross Burn where it flows to join the Irthing at Gilsland. Another small fort, of the same design as Throp, came to light only in 1933 at Boothby, close to the conjectured line of the Stanegate. Before its excavation by F. G. Simpson the only clue to the presence of a Roman site at this place, on a hill (544630) overlooking the Irthing, was the presence of the name 'Castle Hill' on an eighteenth-century estate map. Here is striking proof of the persistence of a place-name long after the field evidence of the fort has been obliterated. But the most fascinating of the Hadrianic forts that were occupied for only a short period at the making of the new frontier stands on the river cliff of the Irthing a mile (one and a half kilometres) to the west of Brampton. It lies at the end of a lane that twists through fields that have given up abundant evidence of a native British settlement of the Roman period. The church of Old St Martin's and its graveyard overlie the north-east corner of the Roman fort, while the rest is occupied by a field. The great eighteenth-century antiquaries of the Roman Wall knew of the site of the fort at Old Church Brampton but its archaeological rediscovery awaited the work of Professor Ian Richmond in 1935, when a turf rampart laid on clay and cobble foundations was uncovered. Two of the lanes that lead down from St Martin's church to the river have also been shown to be of Roman origin. The attractions of Old Church Brampton lie not only in the site of the early Hadrianic fort above the woods and green water meadows of the Irthing, but also its medieval church and shady churchyard contained within the compass of the former rampart. One is led to wonder what meaning the Roman forts along the Stanegate possessed for the founders of medieval churches. Were they places where the wandering missionaries of the sixth and seventh centuries, to whom so many churches of the north and west are dedicated, gathered their congregations in the open air and preached their sermons? Such sites hallowed by the first Christians would then be chosen for the building of a church. Or did the forts at Nether Denton and Old Church Brampton provide only a quarry of building material?

From Gilsland westward the Roman Wall follows a course on the brink of the wooded crags and precipices above the Irthing, until it drops to the lower ground beyond Lanercost. Although this section of the Wall lacks the spectacularly wild scenery of Housesteads, where it winds over the crags of the Whin Sill, the piece to the north of the Irthing contains features of unique interest that have helped to solve some of the major problems in its development. Here, within a distance of two miles (three kilometres), almost every feature of Hadrian's Wall can be illustrated. Along the lane that leads past the site of the fort at Birdoswald (6166) long sections of the Wall are beautifully exposed, the distinctive squared blocks still standing to heights of seven and eight courses. The rubble core, made up of stones of different sizes and shapes and held together by one of the toughest cements invented by man, may be seen in many places. Along the road the repetitive architectural units of the Roman Wall may be examined in detail, and at sites that are

now preserved by the Ministry of Works. The foundations of two milecastles, numbers 50 and 51, survive at High House (607661) and Wall Bowers (593655). In the same length of road the foundations of turrets are exposed at fixed distances of about 500 yards (450 metres) between the milecastles. Across the fields to the south of the lane may be seen the straight grassy rampart of the Turf Wall, much smoothed down by almost two thousand years of exposure to wind and weather. It was in this sector of the Tyne–Solway frontier that archaeology revealed some of the most important facts about the building of Hadrian's Wall, and of the relationship between the Turf Wall and the later rebuilding of the western section in stone. Proof was obtained from a fragment of an inscription found at the site of a milecastle on the Turf Wall that this feature was built in Hadrian's time. Likewise finds from the milecastles along the stone wall near Birdoswald proved that this feature, too, was constructed in Hadrian's time. The realigned stone wall must have been built only a few years after its forerunner.

The most impressive object on Hadrian's Wall in the section between Gilsland and Lanercost is undoubtedly the fort at Birdoswald (6166) (Fig. 1*c*). On the ground one can still trace the outline of this five-acre (two-hectare) fort and in places the boundary wall stands several courses high. The northern edge of Birdoswald abuts on to the line of Hadrian's Wall. Its southern flank lies only a few yards from the steep slopes, scarred with the marks of unrecorded landslips, that plunge two hundred feet (sixty metres) to the valley-floor of the Irthing, where the river twists through woods and pastures. Considered only in strategic terms there are many puzzling features about the site of Roman *Camboglanna* or Birdoswald. If the Roman Wall was designed primarily as a defence against invasion from the north, one might well question the effectiveness of the site of Birdoswald. To the north the ground falls away gently into the shallow depression of Midgeholme

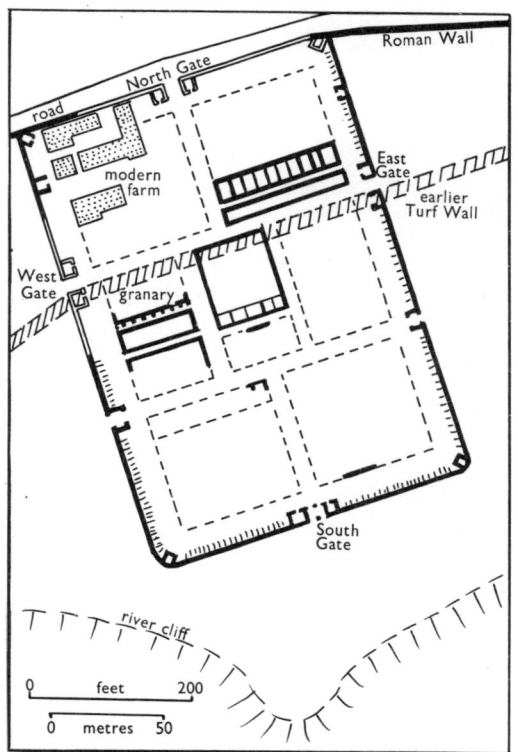

Fig. 1c Birdoswald Fort (after Richmond)

Moss (6166). In this direction Birdoswald commands a limited extent of rising ground. Immediately behind the fort, to the south, the land plunges steeply to the floor of the Irthing. *Camboglanna*, in fact, turns its back on the most valuable strategic feature in its locality, the deep wooded trough followed by the River Irthing. If the function of Hadrian's Wall had been conceived only in strategic terms, a far better course for this frontier would have been drawn to the south of the river, close to the Stanegate and the pre-Hadrianic forts and military posts.

The decisions that determined the details of the topography of the Wall are lost to history; archaeology can only provide clues to the events in northern Britain between A.D. 120 and 130. At least it is clear that the earliest line of Hadrian's forts was placed to the south of the Irthing with sites at Carvoran, Throp, Nether Denton, Boothby Castle Hill and Old Church. At a later date Hadrian's original scheme was modified and the garrison forts were re-established on the line of the Wall. The careful investigation of Birdoswald in the 1930s showed that part of the Wall and a turret had to be destroyed to make way for the fort. The same excavation also uncovered the exciting fact that the Romans were not the first to make use of this high promontory above the Irthing. The traces of a double ditch across the spur at Birdoswald suggest that the native British had constructed a fort there, a view that is strengthened by the discovery of native pottery, suggesting an occupation shortly before the Romans.

Through their thorough archaeological investigation F. G. Simpson and I. A. Richmond have unravelled the stages of the Roman development of the site at Birdoswald. Within the earthwork of the British settlement they discovered a quadrangular enclosure that was probably the foundation of a Roman signal station – a forward lookout post that surveyed back across the river to the fort at Nether Denton. The next stage in the evolution of Birdoswald was the building of the Turf Wall. The foundations of the Turf Wall and its northward-facing ditch have been discovered running across the later fort of *Camboglanna* from east to west. In fact, the eastern and western gates of the rectangular-shaped fort were built over the foundations of the Turf Wall. The most important development in the making of Hadrian's Wall, the building of the large forts, must have taken place soon after the completion of the frontier line in turf. At Birdoswald the archaeologists discovered the remains of a row of open-ended wooden sheds which have been interpreted as builders' temporary shacks erected at the time of the construction of the stone fort. Part of these sheds, it is believed, disappeared in a landslide over the lip of the precipice that falls to the Irthing. One can only speculate upon this minor natural catastrophe that is suggested by the debris uncovered by the archaeologist's spade, but it is not impossible that we have here the faint proof of man's interference with the crude environment of the Irthing Valley. The need for timber in the establishment of the frontier works on the Turf Wall and the later demands for wood in making the fort at Birdoswald, probably resulted in the rapid stripping of woodland on the steep northern flank of the Irthing Valley. As a consequence, the development of gullies in periods of heavy rain, would give rise to minor landslips.

The lineaments of *Camboglanna* have withstood many changes. A farmhouse occupies the north-west corner of the fort and the frontier theme of a later age is repeated in the battlemented pele tower that rises above the roof line. The heart of the Roman fort is now occupied by a rough pasture, a ha-ha, and a garden with a monkey puzzle tree. The tastes and fashion of the early nineteenth century have imposed themselves on this fragment of the border landscape. When Horsley wrote his great survey of the Roman Wall, at the beginning of the eighteenth century, much more was visible on the ground at Birdoswald than meets the eye today. The lines of streets could be made out clearly between the footings of buildings. Birdoswald probably had the richest collection of remains standing above ground of any place along Hadrian's Wall at the beginning of the eighteenth century, but building, road-making and the enclosure of thousands of acres of common land in the early nineteenth century, have taken their toll all along the Roman Wall.

Hadrian's Wall and the Evolution of the Landscape Since Roman Times

The Roman Wall and its related features from the Stanegate forts to the northern outpost at Bewcastle, provided a ground-plan for the later development of the landscape in the region of the Irthing Valley. In many places there is a sense of continuity from Roman times until the present day, particularly where churches have been built within the ramparts of Roman forts at Nether Denton, Old Church Brampton and Bewcastle. But the archaeological record does not strongly support the idea of an unbroken chain of life down the centuries. In the vanished civil settlements outside the forts at Castlesteads and Birdoswald, there is every proof of the extinction of settlements that flourished until the close of the fourth century.

Plate 30   A section of the Roman Wall with its squared facing stones to the east of Birdoswald (NY 6166)

But at Old Church Brampton there is stronger evidence for a continuity of settlement. There, archaeology has yielded abundant proof in coins and pottery of a native settlement to the east of the Roman fort. Air photographs have revealed a network of fields related to this site. Excavation has produced strong evidence of continued occupation after the Romans abandoned northern Britain at the close of the fourth century.

The next stage of settlement history must be worked out from the evidence of place-names. Brampton first appears in the documents in 1169 as *Brantun*, meaning 'the farmstead in the brambly place'. The name probably dates back to the first period of Anglian settlement towards the close of the sixth century. The Irthing Valley with its rich farmland was favoured by the Anglo-Saxons and we find other witnesses of their early settlement in the names of Hayton (5057), Irthington (4961), Farlam (5558) and the Dentons. At Brampton the Anglians probably settled on the site of the present market village, a mile (one and a half kilometres) from the Roman and Dark Age centre. At some time after the beginning of the seventh century this more ancient British settlement, close to the Roman fort, was abandoned and life became focused on the young Anglian foundation at modern Brampton. But the desertion of Old Church Brampton must have taken place after the establishment of the church dedicated to St Martin and built in the corner of the Roman fort. Tradition hallowed the site so it was not until 1781 that the inconvenience of Old Church Brampton, lying a mile and a half (two kilometres) away from the main settlement, was overcome by the building of a new parish church at the centre of the town. Only the chancel of the medieval church of St Martin's was left standing to serve as a mortuary chapel for the cemetery. The stones of the rest of the building were carted away to the new church. The great stimulus to Brampton's growth probably came in 1252, when Thomas de Multon, lord of the Barony of Gilsland, obtained a charter from Henry III to hold there a weekly market and four annual fairs for sheep and cattle. A few decades earlier the founding of a castle, the Mote (533613), had no doubt established the importance of the new site, and perhaps given Brampton the urban character which it has maintained down the centuries.

In studying the history of the landscape around the Irthing Valley one cannot deny the persistence of the Roman framework through the centuries, but there is no easy logic in the values that succeeding generations have placed on the Roman objects which they found in the countryside. For instance, the Roman road system plays little part in the modern communications of the region. The Stanegate, in its course to the south of the Irthing, has been traced only as a result of patient and recent research – and even so, several pieces of the route remain far from certain. Likewise the road that strikes northward from Birdoswald to Bewcastle has little to do with the present network of lanes in the district. Hadrian's Wall, on the other hand, has played an important role in subsequent landscape evolution. For instance on Craggle Hill (5564) and Hare Hill (5664) the Wall acted as the boundary of the deer park that belonged to Lanercost Priory. But in this region the Wall never functions as a parish boundary, despite the fact that this task was often given to Roman roads and other ancient man-made features of the landscape. The most striking function of the Roman Wall in the centuries that followed the withdrawal from the British province, has been as the site of farms. Doubtless, the Wall provided a ready source of building materials. To the west of Birdoswald we find Appletree (597657), Wall Bowers (592655), Leahill (582651), Bankshead (579649), Banks (568646), Hare Hill (563647), and Haytongate (554645) – all placed on the line of the Wall or very close to it. Suddenly between the Irthing's two northern tributaries, the Burtholme Beck (5464) and the King Water (5264), the farms on the Hadrianic frontier are transferred to the line of the Vallum and none occurs on the Wall. We find Howgill (539643), Low Wall (535643) and Dovecote (531642). The top edge of the Vallum served the Romans as a line of communication, and it is not improbable that it was used hundreds of years later, to provide a lane connecting the newly-planted farms.

It is impossible to be certain about the period when farms were first built on the line of the Roman Wall and its parallel southern earthwork, the Vallum. Several make their first appearance in the documents during the seventeenth and eighteenth centuries; others seem to have been medieval foundations. For instance, Leahill (582651) is first recorded in 1702 while Hare Hill (563647), Howgill (539643) and Low Wall (535643) all make their appearance in the seventeenth century. But the names of some of the farms are much older. Banks (568646), a name descriptive of its site on the Roman Wall, is first recorded in 1256. Although the documentary history of a place-name provides a valuable clue to the topographical evolution of a settlement, one must never place too much reliance on the first appearance of a place in the records. Such an entry tells us that a place is in being; it does not necessarily record its beginning. Nevertheless it seems unlikely that any of the farm-sites of the Roman Wall predate the Norman Conquest. Before that time settlements were largely confined to the fertile lower valley of the Irthing. Place-names point to Anglian settlements at Irthington (4961) and Brampton. Burtholme (5463), 'the water-meadow by the river Burt', suggests a settlement that goes back to the spread of Scandinavian farmers in the north-west during the tenth century. Walton (5264) which means 'the settlement by the Wall' is the most striking exception. It is a clustered village on the crest of a spur above the Irthing. Abutting on the Wall from the north, the southern edge of the settlement has obliterated milecastle 56. Walton makes its first documentary appearance in 1169, but the foundation of the village probably took place four or five centuries earlier.

The earliest time at which isolated farms were founded on the Roman Wall was probably in the twelfth and thirteenth centuries – a period when population and the frontiers of settlement were expanding all over western Europe. Not that the Cumbrian border country presented the opportunities of the deep forests of the Weald or the boulder-strewn slopes of Dartmoor about the 1000 foot (300 metres) contour in these expansive centuries. The northern border was disturbed from time to time by hostile raiders, and the isolated farm was a dangerously exposed form of settlement. Nevertheless, the first farmstead at Banks was built in this period of medieval prosperity. For the rest, the farms of the Roman Wall largely date from the seventeenth and eighteenth centuries, when greater security was brought to the border region, and in a period when the large-scale enclosure and improvement of the moors and commons had started.

The Emperor Hadrian created a frontier when the Wall and its web of camps and watch-towers was stretched between the Tyne and the Solway. For fifteen centuries, until the Union of the Crowns in 1601, it was a region of insecurity marked by battlemented farms and pele towers, but the coming of an unbroken peace placed the Wall, as an historic monument, in its greatest danger. Its continuous use as a quarry through the eighteenth century did infinitely more harm than a thousand years of the Pictish invader and the cattle-raiding moss troopers.

Further Reading
Birley, E. *Research on Hadrian's Wall* (1961).
Collingwood, Bruce J. *Handbook to the Roman Wall* 12th edition by I. A. Richmond (1966).
Manning, W. H. 'A hoard of Romano-British ironwork from Brampton, Cumberland' *Transactions of the Cumberland and Westmorland Antiquarian and Archaeological Society* vol. 66 (NS) (1966) pp. 1–36.
Richmond, I. A. and Birley, E. B. 'Excavations on Hadrian's Wall in the Birdoswald-Pike Hill sector, 1929' *Trans. Cumb. and West Antiq. and Arch. Soc.* vol. 3 (NS) (1930) pp. 169–205.
Salway, P. *The Frontier People of Roman Britain* (1965).

Maps
O.S. 1-inch sheet 76 (Carlisle); O.S. 2½-inch sheets NY 56, NY 66, and NY 57. O.S. 2½-inch sheet (Hadrian's Wall).

Suggested Itinerary
A day's excursion may be devoted to an inspection of the Roman Wall to the north of the Irthing Valley between Gilsland (6366) and Castlesteads (5163). Take the Brampton road from Gilsland and begin the excursion where it intersects Hadrian's Wall near the school. Follow the footpath along the Wall to Willowford (625665). The Vallum here runs very close to the Wall. The foundations of a turret are exposed at 629663, and the outline of a temporary Roman Camp – one of

82

Plate 31 Hadrian's Wall at Willowford (NY 6266)

several in the complex of features along the Wall – may be seen on Willowford Hill (625661). On approaching Willowford Farm the cart-road occupies the ditch in front of the Wall, and turret 48B stands up clearly to the left, as one enters the farmyard. Descend to the flood-plain of the Irthing where the remains of the Roman bridge and mill may still be discerned. Note that since the construction of the bridge and mill-race, the river has swung to the west, under-cutting the foot of Harrow Scar (621664). Turn back to Willowford Farm and then follow the foot-path across the Irthing to Underheugh (619662), and climb the cart-track that regains the line of the Roman Wall at milecastle 49 (620664) above Harrow Scar. From Harrow Scar take the footpath along the Wall westward to Birdoswald (615663). From the edge of the promontory at Birdoswald, there is an excellent viewpoint over the Irthing Valley. Take the road from Birdoswald to Banks (5664), for a large part of the distance this is laid over the foundations of the Wall, leaving the ditch clearly exposed to the north. The Turf Wall may be seen clearly from the road as a dark green bank and ditch across the fields to the south. At Appletree barn (596657) it is worth diverging along the cart-road that leads towards Lanerton; after a few yards (metres), in the tiny valley of the Wall Brook, an excellent section of the Turf Wall is exposed. Return to the road, and note the re-union of the lines of the Turf and Stone Walls at milecastle 51, Wall Bowers (593655). A little beyond Wall Bowers, diverge again from the road and follow the track into the floor of the Irthing Valley at Comb Crag, a quarry whose inscriptions show that it was worked by the Romans. Return to the road, and in the next section to Banks, note the siting of farms in relation to the Wall and the Vallum. On Pike Hill (576648), a viewpoint with a wide prospect westward, stood a Roman signal tower that preceded the building of Hadrian's Wall and which looks back to the forts along the Stanegate. The Wall had to make a zig-zag to fit in with the

83

tower and there is a kink in the modern road at this place, a tiny feature of the modern landscape predetermined almost two thousand years ago.

From Banks (5664) to the crossing of the King Water below Walton, the Roman Wall can be followed by a series of footpaths and cart-roads through Hare Hill (563647), Haytongate (553645) and Howgill (539643). At Hare Hill the highest standing piece of the Wall is to be seen reaching 9 feet 10 inches (3 metres). In this section the Wall formed the boundary of Lanercost Abbey's deer park. Hayton-gate is the place where a medieval drove-road crossed the Wall on its way to Laner-cost and a bridge over the Irthing. A diversion to Lanercost is worthwhile to see the twelfth-century priory built almost entirely of stones from the Roman Wall and containing in its fabric altar stones from Birdoswald and milecastle 52. From How-gill (539643) to Dovecote (531642) the footpath shifts from the line of the Wall to the Vallum. Follow the road up the hill to Walton (5264), a rare early Anglian settlement on the line of the Roman frontier. From Walton the Vallum diverges south of the line of Hadrian's Wall to include the fort of Castlesteads (512635). Note the site of this fort on the bluff above the Cam Beck, a site from which all visible features have been obliterated by the making of the gardens of Castlesteads House in 1791.

Field Work
Make a survey of the country on either side of the Irthing between Gilsland and Irthington, and plot on the $2\frac{1}{2}$-inch map the distribution of Roman building-stones in later structures (churches, barns, houses, field boundaries, etc.).

Further Work
Isolated signal towers formed part of the complex system of works on the Tyne-Solway frontier. The foundations of three such towers have been uncovered in the Irthing Valley district, at Mains Rigg (613652), at Pike Hill (577648), and on the slopes of Gillalees Beacon (577718) to the south of Bewcastle. Nothing is known about the height of each tower, but they all rested on solid foundations and were about 20 foot (6 metres) square. It is believed that the towers were higher than the stone Wall which probably reached up 15 feet (nearly 5 metres) to the rampart work and about 20 feet (6 metres in all with the parapet. Assuming that the plat-form of the lookout towers reached to 25 feet (7·5 metres) (a) calculate from the one-inch or $2\frac{1}{2}$-inch maps the chief features of the surrounding countryside that would be visible from each tower (b) name the Roman forts that would be seen from each tower.

2 Inglewood Forest

The Physical Setting

The scenery of the north-east fringe of the Lake District is quite unlike anything found elsewhere in the region. Here, between the enclosing walls of the Skiddaw massif in the west and the equally impressive Pennine Edge in the east, lies the rather featureless terrain that originally formed part of the great Forest of Inglewood. It is a landscape of great regularity dominated by straight roads, broad open acres with large rectangular fields, planted copses and isolated farms, either arranged along the road or set apart in the fields. Only the occasional nucleated settlement like Skelton (4335), with its fourteenth-century church tower and narrow field strips around, provides a link with the more distant past. For the most part, however, it is a landscape of late enclosure created by man for man out of the original forest bounds.

In the west the area is overlooked by the abrupt edge which forms the lower slopes of mountains like Blencathra (3227), Bowscale Fell (3330) and Carrock Fell (3433). Although the rocks here all belong to the Skiddaw Series, they show a great variation over quite small distances. In the south-east lies Blencathra, surrounded by its magnificent set of corries and the more gentle Souther Fell (3528), with its high-level ice marginal channels on its slopes; both are formed of typical black slate. Nearby in Bannerdale (3429) these slates have been toughened by metamorphism, and give rise to the impressive north-east facing Bannerdale Crags. To the north on Bowscale Fell, it is the flags and grits which have been similarly altered, the latter being well seen in the enclosing walls of the corrie of Bowscale Tarn (3331). The deep trench of the Caldew Valley, running into the mountains westwards from Mosedale (3532), is also cut in the grey grits, but on its northern side a fault brings in the igneous rocks of *gabbro* and *granophyre* which form the heart of Carrock Fell (3433). Here, on an exposed top over two thousand feet (six hundred metres) high amidst rocky boulders and crags, the Iron Age people built one of the few hill-forts on the margins of the Lake District. Its height and splendid isolation no doubt gave excellent views over what was to become the Forest of Inglewood in later centuries, and the corridor of the Eden Valley.

All these different rock types have responded to the effects of glaciation and periglaciation. At the height of the glacial period this was an area of considerable ice accumulation and for a long time afterwards, snow and ice would be likely to

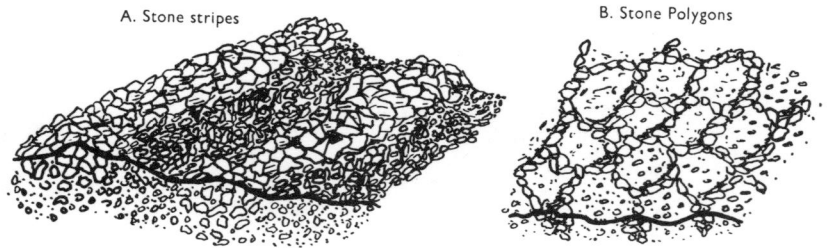

A. Stone stripes   B. Stone Polygons

Fig. 2a   Patterned ground resulting from periglaciation

persist in corries like Bowscale due to the fact that they faced the direction of minimum insolation. They would also be affected by the eddy accumulation of the helm wind on the lee-side of Bowscale Fell. In addition to direct glacial activity the rocks of the Skiddaw massif were susceptible to the action of frost, especially when subject to alternate freezing and thawing. The angular blocks which litter the surface of the top of Bowscale Fell and High Pike have been derived in this way. The same is true of the stone screes which have formed at the foot of crags like those near Mungrisdale (3630), and below Carrock Fell, north of Mosedale (3532). *Periglaciation*, as the whole process is termed, was very active during the closing stages of the Ice Age and afterwards. Even at the present time the process can still take place when the subsoil becomes frozen for a relatively long period during severe winters. One effect is for the angular rock fragments to become arranged in lines to form what are termed *stone stripes* (Fig. 2*a*). A good example of this occurs on the scree of volcanic lava rock fragments forming the north-western flank of High Pike (3135). Somewhat similar is the linear sorting of the extensive slate scree to the north of Blencathra (323277) where the individual stripes are arranged about a foot (thirty centimetres) apart. In between the coarse bands the surface is composed of a clayey loam with small angular slate fragments incorporated in it. The striping represents the result of both internal movements within the upper soil layers following alternate freezing and thawing, and a general soil flow down-slope under gravity. Occasionally, especially on a flat surface such as is found on the top of Blencathra where soil flow or *solifluction* is at a minimum, the stones are arranged to form rough polygons about two feet (sixty centimetres) across with the larger elongated slates encircling a mass of smaller fragments (Fig. 2*a*). The stones tend to be restricted to the surface layers and overlie a bed of clayey loam four to six inches (ten to fifteen centimetres) thick before a further layer of angular rock débris is reached, which passes down to the solid rock below.

In complete contrast to the high country of the Skiddaw massif, the Forest of Inglewood forms a plateau of Carboniferous Limestone. The limestone gives rise to a well-marked scarp overlooking the Mosedale depression at Hutton Roof (3734), but elsewhere it is mainly buried beneath a thick layer of boulder clay, laid down by ice moving through the Eden Valley in a general northerly direction towards the Solway lowland. As a result large areas of the plateau are flat and rather featureless, lacking anything which resembles typical limestone scenery. There are few scars and no limestone pavements such as are found farther south on Crosby Ravensworth Fell where there is a similar outcrop. Instead there is a gradual drop eastwards from a height of about a thousand feet (three hundred metres) in the Hutton Roof area to less than five hundred feet (one hundred and fifty metres) near the Petteril Valley in the east. This reflects the dip of the underlying limestone beds which average between five and ten degrees. The drift cover is so thick, that even when streams have cut deeply into it, they seldom reach the underlying solid rock. In its original state prior to enclosure, the heavy clay gave rise to a climax vegetation of oak woodland making it a natural choice for hunting and sport, the original function of the Forest of Inglewood.

The boundary between the Carboniferous Limestone outcrop and the overlying Penrith Sandstone to the east lies approximately along the line of the Petteril Valley. For the most part the junction is obscured by the thick drift cover, and it is only in parts of the Petteril Valley, as at Crook's Bridge (4448), that the red coloured sandstone with its characteristic millet seed grains, is exposed. Here it has been worked as a building stone, and a small quarry opened up in the face of the river cliff. Beyond the line of the A6, which in this part of the Vale of Eden follows the line of the Roman road making for Carlisle, the Penrith Sandstone outcrop gives rise to a distinct line of hills. Originally there must have been a fairly continuous escarpment facing south-west, but river erosion and later glacial activity have split it up into the isolated hills which dominate this attractive stretch of country bordering on the Eden Valley to the east. The sandstone hills are highest in the south, Penrith Beacon rising to 937 feet (280 metres) (5231) and decrease steadily north so that at Barrock Fell (4647) the height is just over 700 feet (200 metres). At the maximum of the glaciation in the Eden Valley all the hill-tops would be covered with ice, but later the individual hills would emerge and stand out as *nunataks* above the lowland ice-field. As a result their highest parts are mainly free from drift, and rock outcrops are quite common. On the south side of Lazonby Fell, ice erosion has produced steep crags at Scatchmill Scar (5137). Similar plucking by ice has occurred on Penrith Beacon although here deposits of boulder clay have been left behind to give it a *crag and tail* form. Drumlins on the Penrith Sandstone outcrop are restricted to the lower ground, especially around Blaze Fell (4943), but nowhere are they sufficiently concentrated to give rise to a characteristic 'basket of eggs' topography so typical of many parts of the Vale of Eden. Near High Hesket (4744) lies the marshy area of Tarn Wadling, which as its name implies is the site of a former mere.

The Landscape History of Inglewood Forest
Inglewood ranked high among the great forests of medieval England. It was as important as the New Forest or the Forest of Dean and by the reign of Henry II,

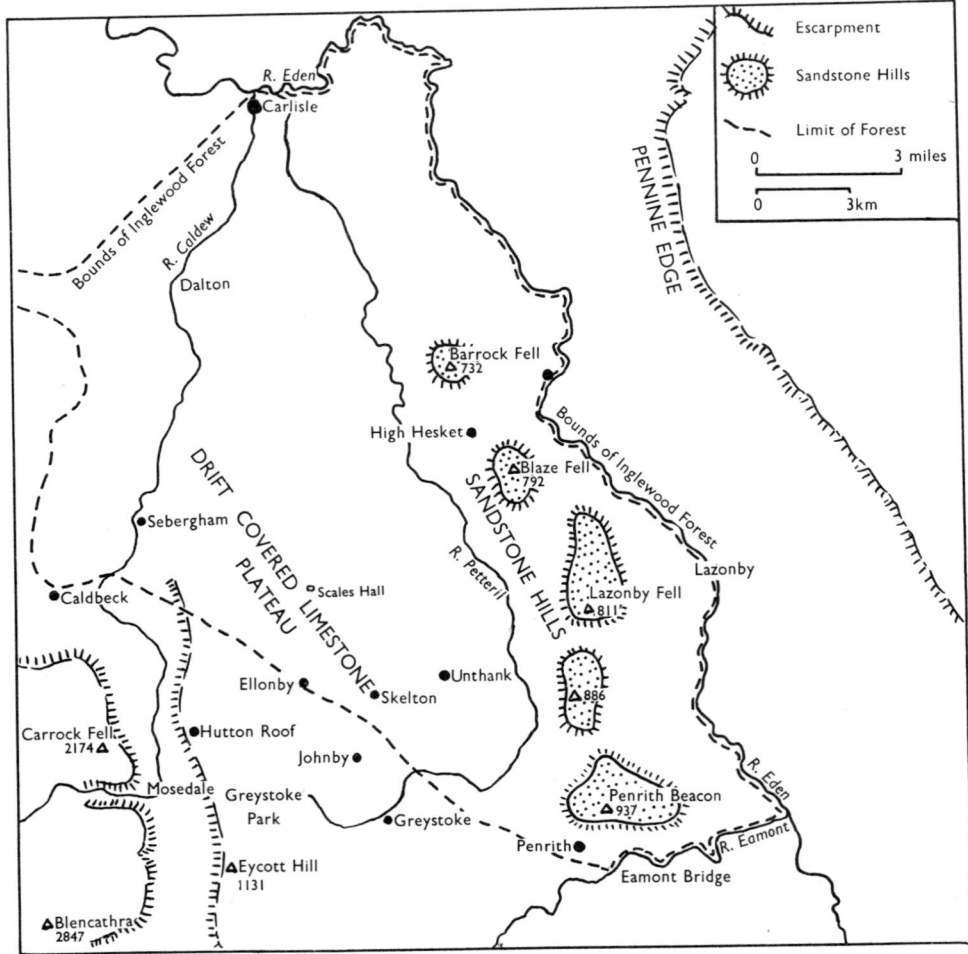

Fig. 2b   Features of Inglewood Forest

when the bounds were extended across the Eden to the Pennines and northwards
to the shores of Solway, Inglewood was the largest of England's hunting preserves.

The boundaries of Inglewood are recorded in detail in the many documents that
deal with the affairs of this royal forest between the thirteenth and sixteenth centuries (Fig. 2*b*). For instance, a perambulation of 1300 spells out its usually accepted
bounds. The eastern limit was marked by the River Eden, from its junction with
the Eamont below Penrith to where it receives the waters of the Caldew at Carlisle.
The northern boundary ran, as the surveyors of Edward I's time reported, from
'the bridge over Caldewe outside the City of Carlisle, along the great metalled way
to Thurseby' and thence to the crossing of the River Wampool. The choice of this
road as a boundary reveals the active role of the chief Roman road westward from
Carlisle, more than a thousand years after it was first driven through the Cumbrian
countryside. The western frontier of Inglewood ran from Wampool Bridge along
the Chalk Beck and under the eastern flanks of the Skiddaw massif to the important
river crossing at Eamont Bridge on the outskirts of Penrith (5228).

88

Like the other royal forests, medieval Inglewood was much more than an empty, uninhabited wilderness, shady with wide-spreading oaks, and the preserve of deer, wild boar and hawks that were always named as the king's own property. Long before William II named Inglewood as a royal forest in the closing decade of the eleventh century, it had contained a number of settlements and the grazing of live-stock in woodland clearings already formed an occupation that was to grow in importance over the next three centuries. The name Inglewood itself means 'the forest of the Angles' and the place-names of some of its oldest settlements show that it was actively colonised from Northumbria during the seventh and eighth centuries. Skelton (4335) first appears in a mid-twelfth-century charter, but the name of Old English origin had probably been coined long before the Norman Conquest. Even today some features of Skelton suggest its early and distinctive role in the landscape history of Inglewood Forest. The settlement has a compact and nucleated form in a district that is typified by hamlets or lonely, isolated farms. The field pattern that surrounds the village on every side with its long, narrow rectangular-shaped enclosures, betrays a vanished system of medieval land-use where farmers shared the intermixed strips (Fig. 2c). The place-name element 'rigg', usually indicative of a former open field system, still survives in Kirk Rigg (441359) and High Rigg (440346). At Skelton a farming community working the wide acres of its open fields must have been planted within Inglewood Forest, long before the Norman Conquest. Dalston (3650) too was another early nucleus of settlement. Its documentary history begins in 1187, but the name itself, coined several centuries earlier, probably contains the Old English personal name *Deall*. Dalston then is 'Deall's farm or settlement', and it most likely commemorates the clearing of a tract of the wilderness of Inglewood Forest twelve hundred years ago. The bounds of the royal forest of Inglewood contained not only the villages of Anglian farmers who had made their way across the Pennines into the Eden Valley, but to the south lay an ancient nucleus of British settlement at Penrith, and within its northern boundary stood the regional capital of the north-west, Carlisle.

Fig. 2c   Contrasting field patterns in Inglewood

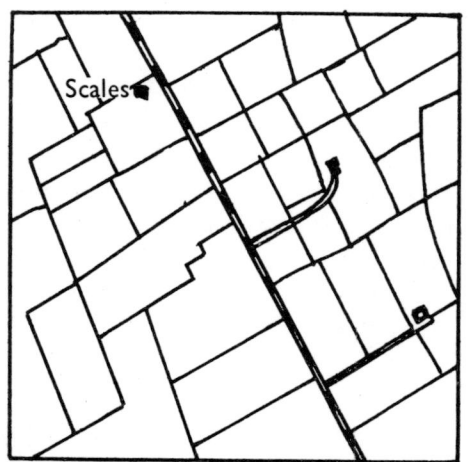

The centuries between the Norman Conquest and the accession of the Tudors are rich with documents relating to Inglewood Forest and its management. Two opposing trends are revealed in the history of the landscape. First, there is the desire to retain this tract as a hunting preserve, an aim that underlies the innumerable reports of trials and investigations that sought to apply the code of the 'forest laws'. Against those who wished to perpetuate the wilderness, there pressed a silent army of colonising farmers, illegally carving out new pastures and patches of arable from the forest. Perhaps the most striking attempt to preserve the wilderness was the making of Plumpton Hay (4835) by William II, in the closing years of the eleventh century. An extensive tract of land between the River Petteril and the eastern bounds of Skelton was fenced off as a royal deer park. Plumpton Park, as this enclosure of some 2500 (1000 hectares) was later called, remained a royal deer park until Henry VIII's reign when the first farmers were encouraged to settle within its limits. Camden, the great Elizabethan topographer, has preserved a vivid account of the late settlement of this piece of Inglewood Forest. 'Upon the banks of Petril lies Plumpton Park (once called the Haja de Plumpton) very large, and formerly set apart by the kings of England for the keeping of deer, but by King Henry VIII prudently planted with men, being almost a frontier between England and Scotland'. Even today the landscape between Hutton-in-the-Forest and the valley of the Petteril suggests a district of late settlement with its rare and widely scattered farms, a pattern of moderate-sized and square-shaped fields, and an absence of any settlement that can be described as a nucleus.

If Henry VIII felt that the nearness of the Scots frontier was a reason for the colonisation of the empty lands of Plumpton Hay, the same motive of national security coloured the Crown's attitudes to Inglewood Forest in earlier centuries. Soon after William II's conquest of north-western England and the occupation of Carlisle in 1092, the same king deliberately planted colonists from Normandy and Flanders on the lands of Inglewood Forest to increase the security of the dangerous northern marches. A number of these Norman settlements are gathered in the northern fringe of the Forest, on the outskirts of Carlisle. They can all be recognised by their Norman personal names attached to the element *by* which means a 'settlement'. For instance, in a ring to the south of Carlisle we find Upperby (Hubert's *by*), Harraby (Henry's *by*) and Etterby (Etard's *by*). A little farther to the east the tiny 'street village' of Aglionby (4456) dates from the same period of settlement in the twelfth century. The first element of the place-name stems from *Agyllun*, a Norman-French personal name. It is not impossible that this particular founder of a settlement in Inglewood Forest is named among the twelfth-century charters of Wetheral Abbey where a Lawrence, son of Agyllun, is recorded as holding a piece of land at Aglionby in 1176. An earlier document, dated to the year 1130 or 1131, records the name of a Walter Agullon, who was one of the witnesses of a charter of Hildred of Carlisle to the monks of Wetheral. It seems not unlikely

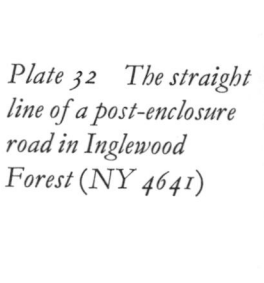

Plate 32   The straight
line of a post-enclosure
road in Inglewood
Forest (NY 4641)

that this Walter Agullon was the founder of the new settlement at Aglionby, and
that we may date this little colony to the years about A.D. 1130.

Another group of settlements, deliberately planted by the Normans, appeared
on the southern fringe of Inglewood Forest in the early years of the twelfth century.
Lamonby (4135), Ellonby (4235) and Johnby (4333) were all intruded into the
empty western quarter of Skelton parish, where the land begins to climb steeply
towards the bleak limestone summit of Greystoke Forest. The hamlets of these
twelfth-century settlers from the Continent are still distinguished by the orderly
line of farmsteads arranged in a linear pattern along one side of the road. The *Pipe
Rolls*, documents that record the affairs of royal estates, contain evidence for the
advance of the frontier of farming into Inglewood. There are numerous grants of
plots of land, none of them very large, to individual farmers hidden behind the
references to *purprestures* and *assarts*. A 'purpresture' meant the building of a house
or shelter while an 'assart' describes a deliberate clearing of the forest for cultivation. Sometimes grants of larger tracts of land were made to important individuals
or families so that they could encourage the enclosure and development of their
newly acquired properties. In 1317 John de Penrith was granted a lease of land at
Braithwaite on the banks of the River Ive (4242). Another reference in the Pipe
Rolls for 1381 shows how Richard Trotter was given a grant 'to enclose and hold
10 acres of land between Todholgill and Blakebeck, and the closes of Morton and
Wollaykes, and to build a lodge there' (4439).

The Middle Ages witnessed the piecemeal enclosure and improvement of much
of Inglewood Forest. The last great survey of the bounds of the royal forest was
made in 1380. From the end of the fourteenth century it can be claimed that farming had overwhelmed the claims of the huntsman in Inglewood. This long process
of settlement is itself written on the contemporary landscape. Perhaps the centuries
of medieval colonisation are nowhere better summed up than in the history of

Plate 33   Mellguards Farm, Inglewood Forest. The Petteril valley lies in the middle distance, and beyond is the discontinuous scarp of the Penrith Sandstone (NY 4446)

Sebergham (3641). In their great *History of Cumberland*, written at the end of the eighteenth century, Nicholson and Burn look back to the time of the Norman Conquest and describe Sebergham as 'a great waste and wilderness'. They attribute its development to a hermit, William de Wastedale, who established a cell there on a hill above the Caldew about 1180, and who 'began to enclose some part of it'. A century later, in 1285, the story of the growth of Sebergham is taken up again in one of the largest primary sources of information on Inglewood Forest, the great roll of the *Pleas of the Forest*. It surveys the affairs of the royal forest over the previous quarter of a century, and vividly describes the expansion of Sebergham and its establishment as a separate parish. 'They say further that whereas the King had a certain free chapel in the said forest in a place called Sebergham, and a chantry of one chaplain there for the King and his ancestors, it is now turned into a mother church, worth 20 marks a year . . . and there is made a great town where there used to be one house and no more'.

The central part of the Forest between the Petteril and the Caldew became an extensive tract of open, unfenced common grazing land, after the Tudor dis-afforestation extinguished the rights of the huntsman. The final shaping of the landscape of Inglewood was achieved by a succession of Enclosure Acts that fill the history of the eighteenth century. Five thousand acres (two thousand hectares) of common were enclosed at Castle Sowerby in 1769, and the six hundred acres (two hundred and fifty hectares) of Johnby Common disappeared under a network of hedges in 1783. But the greatest change in the landscape was achieved by the *Enclosure Act* for Inglewood Forest that was awarded by Parliament in 1819. It was

92

Plate 34   The rectangular pattern of fields in Inglewood Forest created by the Enclosure Award of 1819 (NY 4238) Aerofilms

applied to 28,000 acres (11,000 hectares) of common land and in the ensuing years of the 1820s a grid of long straight enclosure roads, formal rectangular fields, neat hedgerows planted with trees, neatly sown spinneys and isolated cottages and farms took the place of the ragged unkempt wilderness, that was the last remnant of a noble hunting forest (Fig. 2c). This unmistakable landscape of the Georgian encloser, working to the detailed instructions of the Parliamentary Award, may be explored to the north of Skelton (4338) and again at Broad Field (4244), westward of Southwaite. As the enclosure of the old common grazing land went forward and the new fields were ploughed up for farming, the nineteenth-century pioneers reported evidence of their medieval forerunners in the district, in the shape of scores of pits where charcoal had been burnt from the huge forest oaks.

Further Reading

Graham, T. H. B. 'Skelton' *Transactions of the Cumberland and Westmorland Antiquarian and Archaeological Society* vol. xxx (NS) (1930) pp. 27–43.

Graham, T. H. B. 'Englewood' *Trans. Cumb. and West. Antiq. and Arch. Soc.* vol. xxxiii (NS) (1933) pp. 15–23.

Parker, F. H. M. 'Inglewood Forest', a series of valuable articles in seven parts in the *Trans. Cumb. and West. Antiq. and Arch. Soc.* vols. v–xi (NS) (1905–11).

Parker, F. H. M. 'The development of Inglewood', *Trans. Cumb. and West. Antiq. and Arch. Soc.* vol. xii (NS) (1912) pp. 1–28.

Shackleton, E. H. *Lakeland Geology* (1966).

Tate, W. E. 'A hand list of English Enclosure Acts and Awards' *Trans. Cumb. and West. Antiq. and Arch. Soc.* vol. xliii (NS) (1943) pp. 175–98.

Maps

O.S. 1-inch sheets 76 (Carlisle), 83 (Penrith); O.S. 2½-inch sheets NY 43.

Suggested Itinerary

Most of the themes in the landscape history of Inglewood Forest may be illustrated on a wandering traverse between Penrith (5130) and Sebergham (3541). Take the road B5305 as far as Skelton (4335). With the aid of the 2½-inch map, examine the field pattern around this nucleated settlement. An excellent impression of a former open field and the distinctive pattern of its later enclosure can be gained from the lane that leads from the church across Kirk Rigg (4435) to Unthank (4536), a place-name which means 'against the will'. Here it refers to an illegal squatter settlement on the fringes of Skelton that first appears in the documents in 1274. The line of widely spaced farms today is suggestive of assarts made in the edge of the forest.

Return to Skelton and make a diversion westward through Ellonby (4235), Johnby (4333) and Lamonby (4135), originally planted settlements of the early years of the twelfth century. Look at the post-enclosure features of the landscape between Skelton and Middlesceugh (4041) and conclude the excursion at Sebergham (3641) in a parish that emerged from the process of settlement in the thirteenth century.

Field Work

(*a*) With the aid of the 2½-inch map sheet NY 43 plot the individual drumlins which occur in the country south of Skelton. Using measurements from the map, make a graph to show the relationship between their length and height.

(*b*) With the help of the 2½-inch map, sheet NY 43, trace out on the ground the probable former limits of the open fields of Skelton (4335).

Further Work

Using the 2½-inch map, sheet NY 43, as your source, attempt to map the former extent of open fields in this area. Note that the boundaries of the enclosed strips show as bunches of narrow rectangles, and frequently the longer sides are gently curved.

3 The Lead-mining Landscape of Alston Moor

Alston has the unenviable distinction of being the highest market town in England. Set on a steeply sloping hillside, at a height of just about a thousand feet (three hundred metres), in the angle formed by the valleys of the South Tyne and Nent, it would have remained little more than a moorland hamlet but for the presence of rich lead-bearing veins which brought wealth and prosperity to this inhospitable region. Admittedly Alston Moor lies in the lee of Cross Fell and therefore escapes some of the extreme climatic conditions of the latter area. Even so the area can be almost completely isolated for days on end during the winter months, one reason why the branch railway line from Haltwhistle has been retained as a social necessity. When Hutchinson, the Cumberland topographer, referred to the area at the end of the eighteenth century, he did so in the most depressing terms.

> Alston is a small market town, meanly built, situated at the declivity of a steep hill, inhabited by miners. The fatigue of passing bad roads was in no sense alleviated by the scene which presented itself here. Pent in a narrow valley, over which mountains frowned with a melancholy sterility and nakedness: the wind tempestuous, impending clouds stretching forth a dark and disconsolate curtain over the face of the morning, rain beating vehemently against the windows, which were not able to resist the storm; a few trees standing near the inn tossed by the heavy blasts which howled down the valley; such were the objects which presented themselves to us at Alston. . . . We might be bold to challenge Derbyshire or even Cornwall to produce so peculiarly wild a spot as Alston Moor.

With such inherent climatic disadvantages this area had naturally always been marginal from a farming standpoint. The impetus given by the lead industry, however, both in providing a market and encouraging the development of smallholdings run by miners on a part-time basis, meant that large areas were brought under cultivation, especially following the Enclosure Acts of the early nineteenth century. Hutchinson's view that 'the earth here scarcely produces anything, except from its bowels and the people are subterraneous' was now in need of modification. The landscape in the vicinity of Alston bears clear evidence, even at the present time, of the impact of improvement on a region which had earlier been

95

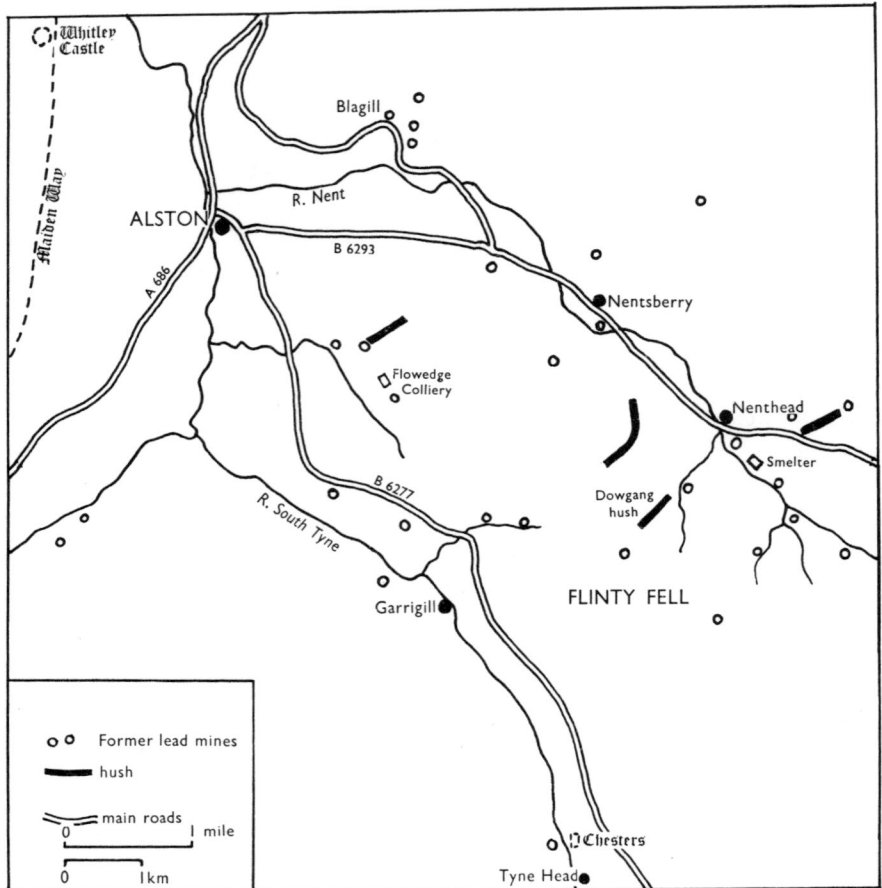

Fig. 3a   The lead-mining areas of Alston Moor

dismissed as hostile and only fit for sheep pasture. Alston, in consequence, not only had its miners in lodging-houses but also its influx of farmers on each market day. Its small market-place, really only a broadening of the cobbled main street and perched half-way down the hillside on which the town is built, must have hummed with activity in times of mining prosperity, when money was freely spent on goods and in the local inns. The main market was on a Saturday but there were sheep and cattle fairs in March, May, September, October and November. During the height of mining activity in the surrounding fells in the mid-nineteenth century, money was available for improving the town. A main water supply was brought from a spring on Broad Pothill and gas lighting came as early as 1843. The medieval church of St Augustine was entirely rebuilt in 1870 at a cost of £4500 while a new Town Hall had been completed in 1858. Both buildings still dominate the town and serve as a reminder of the wealth that once came from lead mining.

It seems probable that lead mining began in the Alston Moor area during Roman times, for pieces of lead ore and even slag have been found in the Roman Camp of Whitley Castle (6948), two miles (three kilometres) north-west of Alston (Fig. 3*a*).

96

Plate 35   Dowgang Hush, by the side of the Nenthead to Garrigill road as it climbs over Flinty Fell (NY 7742)

The camp lies astride the Roman road known as the Maiden Way which traverses the western fringes of the Alston Moor. The road, probably along the line of an older British trackway, functioned primarily as a link between the Roman centre of *Bravoniacum* (Kirkby Thore) in the Eden Valley and the Roman Wall near Greenhead. Its mere presence, however, must have meant that this corner of the Pennines was more accessible than most parts, so that if lead was found it would be relatively easy to exploit and transport to developing Roman towns like *Corstopitum* (Corbridge) not far away. It has even been hinted, by Raistrick, that a Roman mining site existed not far away in the upper reaches of the South Tyne Valley. The site, aptly named Chesters, lies on the valley floor close to the right bank of the river, approximately half-way between Hole House Farm and Tynehead (7638). Nothing much in the way of tangible remains is to be seen, apart from an area of rumpled ground which might represent shallow workings in the river terrace gravels, certainly the most accessible source of lead without recourse to full-scale mining.

Although final proof of Roman lead working in the Alston Moor area must await the results of future research and possibly chance finds, the pattern of development becomes clearer in medieval times when written evidence is available. The interest at that time was in part connected with the silver found with the lead, and as the Crown was involved, there are many references in the *Pipe Rolls, Close Rolls* and the *Calendar of Patents* from 1130 onwards to the mines of Alston. Their exact location is unknown, but the references may well be to mineral veins being worked in the upper part of the South Tyne Valley in the vicinity of Garrigill (7441). Although Alston was the main centre at this time, as it was during the later phases of mining – there is a record of a church in existence at the time of Henry II – many of the miners lived simply in rough huts of turf walls and thatched reed roofs, out on the open moor close to the actual mine workings. Here they were a virtually independent community electing their own officials to administer the

97

basic elements of law and order. Prospecting for lead was a haphazard affair and luck played a considerable part in finding rich ore veins. The practice of *hushing*, involving ponding up water behind an artificial dam high up on the hillside and then releasing the pent up force which would cut a deep gash through the surface soil and thus expose any lead vein, was perhaps the most scientific method of prospecting. Former 'hushes' still scar the hillsides of the Alston area. In the Nent Valley, for example, Greengill Hush (7643) above Holmfoot Farm and Dowgang Hush, close to the mountain road from Nenthead to Garrigill (7742), are but two examples.

Few mining enterprises have made a greater impact on the landscape and life of the Alston region than the London Lead Company, a Quaker organisation whose founding dates back to 1692, when it received a Royal Charter. Their interest in the mineral wealth of this area began in 1706, when they acquired some mines in the headwaters of Brown Gill near the summit of Flinty Fell (7642). Still later they expanded their interest considerably when they leased from Greenwich Hospital the former estates of the Earl of Derwentwater, which he had to forfeit to the Crown, after the unsuccessful rebellion of 1715. The London Lead Company was now established as the biggest operator in the area, and in 1745 they bought the smelt mill at Nenthead (7843) which had been built eight years earlier at a cost of £900. This upper part of the Nent Valley was now becoming the main centre of lead mining following the discovery of the Rampsgill vein, which contained ore of exceptional richness. With their Quaker background, the London Lead Company always had the welfare of their employees very much at heart, and so in 1753 they began to build the first true mining village of the region on a site alongside their Nenthead mines (Fig. 3*b*). Previously miners had either lived in Alston or lodged in farms near the site of the mines. A few may still have continued the medieval

Fig. 3b   Nenthead, as it appeared at the beginning of the century

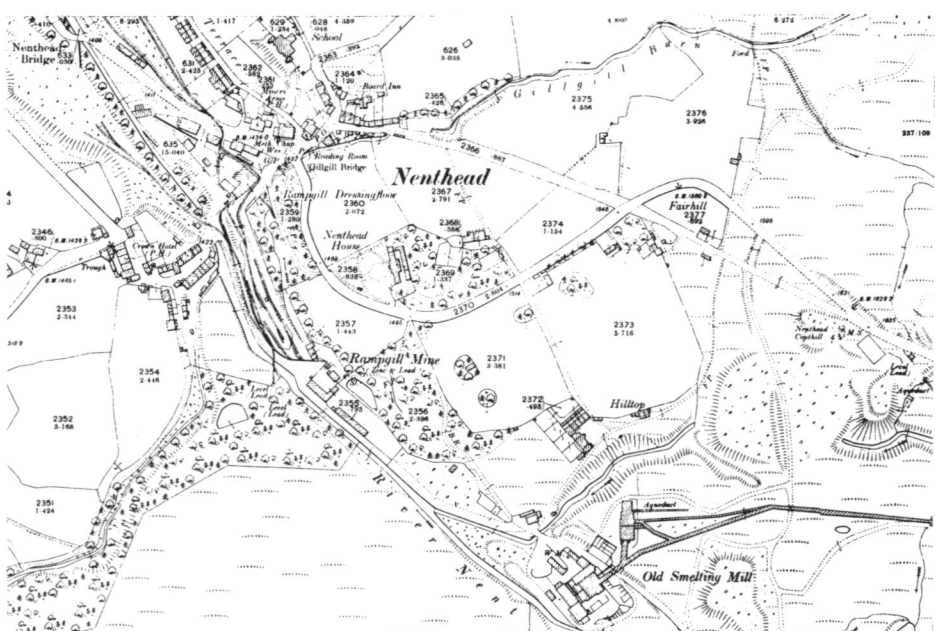

Plate 36 The heart of Nenthead with the former Miners' Arms and chapels still surviving while the evidence of lead-working and smelting is swept away (NY 4337)

practice of living in primitive shielings of turf and rushes on the open moor. This pattern was to alter significantly after 1760, when the first buildings began to spring up at Nenthead to give accommodation for smelters and mine officials. The cottages, in groups of four, were built of local stone and roofed with thick sandstone slabs. Most have now gone or have been substantially restored, though one still has the initials L.L. and date 1766 above the doorway. This part of the village, with its cobbled streets flanked by some old cottages with their uneven roof line, must be part of the original settlement founded by the London Lead Company, though some extensive rebuilding took place in 1825. At this time thirty-four new cottages were built together with a ready-money shop, bath-house, chapel, church and school. The Company, anxious to exercise a moral influence over its workers, had earlier purchased the old inn of the Miner's Arms (now the Nent Head Hotel). Across the river lay the 'suburb' of Overwater which still retains its colour-washed cottages set haphazardly without much thought of planning, perhaps typical of a rapidly growing mining hamlet.

Some idea of the scale of development which had taken place in the latter half of the eighteenth century can be gauged from the fact that in 1766 there were 119 mines producing ore worth £61,950. Money was thus available for further development and investment in new mining techniques. In 1769 the Company purchased cast-iron rails for making waggon-ways from its mines. The biggest operation at this time was the building of an underground level or *sough* to drain the existing mines in the Nent Valley and allow deeper working. The Company called in the eminent engineer, John Smeaton, to carry out their plans. He began tunnelling in 1776 and when his level was completed many years later, it ran for almost five miles (eight kilometres) from the Brewery Shaft above Nenthead village to Alston. Not only did the Nent Force Level serve as a drain, but as it was lined with stone and in its lower section had a depth of four feet (one and a quarter metres) it acted as an underground canal on which 30 foot (9 metre) barges used to ply, carrying away the lead ore. Half-way along its length there was a difference of level of 210 feet (60 metres) between the upper and lower sections and an artificial waterfall linked the two. This later became something of a tourist attraction, and visitors were taken by barge from Alston to see the wonders of the underground Lady-shield Fall. With the collapse of the mining industry in the present century, this remarkable piece of eighteenth-century engineering ceased to have any real purpose. Today its western end, near Alston, has been sealed so that the present day visitor can no longer enjoy the same excitement of an underground voyage by barge as could his Victorian predecessor.

The London Lead Company, in addition to providing employment for hundreds of miners in this inhospitable region and taking a close interest in their welfare, was also instrumental in improving farming and breaking down the isolation of the area through building new roads. Miners were encouraged to take to farming as an insurance policy against periods when slumps occurred in the mining indus-try. This was not too difficult, as an interest in farming had often been aroused when miners lodged with local farmers during the early days of mining. Cottages were built by the Company and rented to the miner. Each had about six acres (two hectares) of land which could be worked as a small-holding, with about fifty acres (twenty hectares) of open pasture for grazing. Most miners living in this way kept a few cows and a small flock of sheep which provided some income when mining fortunes were at a low ebb. Land which normally would have remained as open fell was thus enclosed, and today the landscape of Alston Moor still retains the evidence of the intake of marginal areas up to heights of 1700 feet (500 metres). Farms like Blagillhead (7448) at 1550 feet (465 metres) and Middle Farm (7445) at 1525 feet (457 metres) were sited close to the limits of enclosure, near the fell top. Much of this marginal land has now fallen out of cultivation, and is quickly revert-ing to 'natural' moorland. Stone walls, now broken in many places, still point to man's endeavour to tame this wilderness and wrest some return from its thin acid soils to supplement the variable income from mining. Life must have been extremely harsh at these altitudes, with the only compensation being the chance find of a rich ore strike. The winter was a particularly trying season with deep snows and biting winds sweeping across moors from which the original tree cover had long since been removed. Fortunately some local coal was available in thin seams within the Carboniferous Limestone, and this was exploited in shallow drift workings. One has survived to the present day, Flowedge Colliery (7344) in the valley of Natrass Gill.

The relative isolation of the lead mining valleys around Alston Moor inevitably meant that it was particularly difficult to transport the lead ore to distant smelters or even to bring in food supplies for the growing mining population, in the early years of the nineteenth century. Roads across the moor were virtually non-existent and transport was therefore largely dependent on teams of twelve to fifteen ponies – *galloways* – which used the roughest tracks. One such 'carrier way' ran northwards from Nenthall (7545) in the Nent Valley across Allendale Common, and then dropped down into the valley of the West Allen. Each galloway could only transport about two tons of ore and the route across the top was often impassable in winter. Faced with these difficulties Greenwich Hospital, who owned the lands of Alston Moor, brought in John McAdam, the foremost road engineer of the day, to make a survey for road improvement and new construction in the area. McAdam's suggestions were put into effect, and work began in 1824 on improving the whole line of the main through-road from Hexham to Alston and then across to Penrith.

Throughout the first half of the nineteenth century, in spite of short periods of recession and inactivity, the mining carried out by the London Lead Company brought considerable prosperity to the Alston area. The lead miners, unlike the colliers, were independent and thrifty. A writer of the time noted that:

> they were civil, industrious and intelligent, and show, by the dialect they speak, very little communication with the world beyond their own dales. On a house-to-house visitation I found everything clean, whole and in its place; no trumpery little ornaments as in the collier's cottage. Where there is a picture it is that of some favourite minister, such as Wesley. . . . There are no cheap periodicals or people's editions – they are not reckoned at all canny. The miners like everything good of its kind.

Their income reflected the demand for lead and the price it could fetch on the open market in face of world competition. In good years like those of the 1820–30 decade, production averaged nearly 10,000 tons a year. In the 1830s, increased competition from lower-priced lead from Spain, led to a substantial drop in output. The London Lead Company were forced to cut production by 20 per cent and its labour force by 40 per cent to economise. Recovery came slowly but by 1849–50 the Alston Moor mines recorded their highest level of production. The richer veins, however, were now becoming exhausted, and new sources more difficult to find. This, combined with increased competition from many parts of the New World, brought a crisis in the fortunes of the London Lead Company from 1870 onwards from which it never recovered. There was little work now for miners and those without a supplementary income from farming were forced to leave the area. The population of Alston area fell from 5680 in 1871 to 4621 a decade later. Comparable figures for Nenthead are 1811 to 1419. By 1882 the situation was so serious that the London Lead Company decided to pull out, after almost two hundred years of mining, and so it relinquished its mineral rights over the whole area. This undoubtedly marked the end of an era, for the Company had always been

a considerable social influence as well as providing the main means of livelihood.

The withdrawal of the London Lead Company did not bring mining activities completely to an end, for there were always those who thought they could succeed where others had failed. The Nenthead and Tynedale Company now took over the leases, but in 1896 they sold out to the Vieille Montagne Zinc Company of Belgium who were anxious to exploit the zinc ores. This they did with great success, and in 1902 the Nenthead mines alone produced 8000 tons of zinc blende. New shafts were sunk and a new smelter built in the valley in 1910. When the local supplies of zinc blende ran out, the Company developed new sources in the area of Nentsberry Crags (7645) lower down the valley. Between 1923 and 1938 almost a quarter of a million tons of unconcentrated ore were obtained. The industry was now faced with severe competition from cheaper imported ore, and in 1947 the Vieille Montagne Company closed its mines in the area. Although there has been some sporadic working of old tips since, lead mining has given way almost entirely to fluorspar extraction.

Nenthead today reflects the passing of the mining industry. The smelter upstream from the village now lies derelict, a mass of rubble with only the barest traces of the settling tanks, the hearths and repair shops. Towering above lies one of the great spoil tips, perhaps the most tangible monument to the wealth that once came from the earth below. Up on the fell top lies the other monument to the industry, Killhope Chimney which lay at the end of a long flue, which once carried the lead vapours for half a mile (nearly one kilometre) away from the smelter. In the village, though the cottages are still in good repair, there is a similar air of abandonment, with levelled ground where the washing floors once stood. The substantial chapel, church and school, all belonging to an era when mining was at its peak, now look out of place in the centre of a dwindling community. And yet

Plate 38 Nenthead smelter, gradually disintegrating into a mass of rubble like the spoil heaps around (NY 7843)

as in many other former mining areas, sufficient remains to allow the visitor to conjure up something of the sense of purpose which must have hung over the place, when the mining industry was at its peak. The surrounding hillsides, too, share this impression for the deeply-scored hushes and bare spoil tips which spew their débris out of the mine shafts and adits, are all part of the same story, of man wrestling with hostile forces of nature to create a flourishing mining community in this extreme eastern corner of Cumberland.

Further Reading

Bulmer, T. F. *History, Topography and Directory of East Cumberland* (1884).

Dunham, K. C. *Geology of the Northern Pennine Orefield* vol. 1 (1948).

Davies-Shiel, M. and Marshall, J. D. *The Industrial Archaeology of the Lake Counties* (1969).

Hunt, C. J. *The Lead Miners of the Northern Pennines* (1970).

Raistrick, A. and Jennings, B. *A History of Lead Mining in the Pennines* (1965).

Smailes, A. E. 'The Lead Dales of the Northern Pennines' *Geography,* vol. 21 (1936) pp. 120–9.

Maps

O.S. 1-inch sheets 83 (Penrith) and 84 (Teesdale); O.S. 2½-inch sheets NY 73, and NY 74.

Suggested Itinerary

Alston forms a convenient centre to explore the former lead-mining areas of the neighbourhood. From the town the route eastwards along the south side of the Nent Valley (B6293 road) should be taken. The relatively rich farming which can take place on the valley side slopes opposite, at heights well above a thousand feet (three hundred metres), should be noted. Where the side valley of Blagill enters from the north (7447) terrace features are especially marked, with the harder lime-stone beds and Whin Sill forming the risers, and the softer intervening shales the treads. At Nentsbérry (7645) the cleared site marks the former Haggs mine which was worked during a late phase of mining activity. Farther upstream at Nenthead 7843) lay the principal centre of mining and smelting activity associated with the London Lead Company, who built the industrial hamlet at this convergence of several valleys. From Nenthead the steep mountain road south of the village leads across the neighbouring valley of the South Tyne. By the side of the road the former hush and surface mine of Dowgang can be clearly seen on the way up to the fell top. Descending to Garrigill (7441) other former mine sites are apparent in the valley of the Garrigill Burn and Brown Gill on the western slopes of Flinty Fell (7642). Garrigill village consists of a collection of farms and former miners' cottages, set around a triangular green. It formed a small centre for the mining community of the South Tyne area. From Garrigill the minor road up the valley can be taken until it peters out, close to the now abandoned hamlet of Tyne Head (762380). Between here and Hole House Farm lies the reputed site of Roman lead workings on the river terrace, whose gravel deposits provided the lead. From Tyne Head it is necessary to re-trace the route back to Garrigill and thence by the B6277 road to Alston.

Further Work
The varying fortunes of the lead mining industry of Alston Moor can be followed in the population returns for the area from 1801 to the present day. The data below refers to the parish of Alston together with chapelries of Garrigill and Nenthead:

Year	Population	Year	Population
1801	4746	1891	3384
1811	5078	1901	3134
1821	5699	1911	3075
1831	6858	1921	3334
1841	6062	1931	2678
1851	6816	1939	2889
1861	6404 (incl. 2039 at Nenthead)	1951	2327
1871	5680 (incl. 1811 at Nenthead)	1961	2105
1881	4621 (incl. 1419 at Nenthead)		

The figures can be plotted on a graph, which should also show the main periods of mining activity.

Bibliography of additional references

Barringer, J. C. *Lakeland Landscape: A Geographical Approach* Dalesman 1970

Garlick, T. *Romans in the Lake Counties* Dalesman 1970

Howard, Peter *Birdoswald Fort on Hadrian's Wall* Cameo Books 1969

Marshall, J. D. *Old Lakeland* 1971

Marshall, J. D. and Shiel, M. Davies- *The Industrial Archaeology of the Lake Counties* 1969

Marshall, J. D. and Shiel, M. Davies- *The Lake District at Work: Past and Present* David & Charles 1970

Millward, R. and Robinson, A. *The Lake District* Eyre & Spottiswoode 1970

Pevsner, N. *Cumberland and Westmorland* The Buildings of England Series Penguin 1970

Rollinson, W. *History of man in the Lake District* Dent 1967

Smith, K. *Carlisle* Old Towns and Cities Dalesman 1970

Wade, H. O. *The Pennine Way* H. O. Wade 1966

Index